Transparent Computers

Transparent Computers

Designing Understandable Intelligent Systems

Erik T. Mueller

Publisher: Erik T. Mueller
Version: 2016-01-14 07:28

Contents

1. Introduction

Computers today can be very opaque:

> Jessica selects a medium pizza with mushrooms, enters her credit card information, and hits submit. The computer responds, "An error has occurred."

Given this response, Jessica doesn't know what the exact problem is or how to fix it. Has her credit card been stolen? Should she call her credit card company? Is the pizza restaurant closed? Computers should be more transparent, open, and understandable.

1.1. Transparent Computers

The operation of computers—or devices, systems, programs, or applications—shouldn't be mysterious. They shouldn't use exotic or inscrutable methods. Instead, their operation should be *transparent* or understandable to people. We should be able to understand why they arrived at a particular conclusion or why they behaved in a certain way.

Computers should reason like people. They should use concepts familiar to people and combine them in ways that make sense to people. A transparent computer might reason as follows:

> If the transaction amount is greater than the available credit, then the transaction is declined. The transaction amount is greater than the available credit. Therefore, the transaction is declined.

Computers should explain their reasoning to people. A transparent computer might explain its reasoning to Jessica as follows:

> "Your transaction has been declined," the computer says.
>
> "Why?" Jessica asks.
>
> "Because the transaction amount is $11.75, and your available credit is $7.24."

Computers should engage in dialogues with people. If Jessica isn't satisfied with the explanation, then she can ask for more information:

> Jessica asks, "Why is my available credit $7.24?"
>
> The computer replies, "Because your total credit limit is $5000, your current balance is $4838.49, and you have $154.27 in pending charges."

The computer can also help Jessica solve the problem:

> "What should I do?"
>
> "You can increase your available credit by making a credit card payment, or you can use another credit card."

Computers should learn by interacting with people. When a computer is missing a word, phrase, or piece of knowledge, we should be able to add it through dialogue:

> The computer asks, "Do you live in a city, town, or village?"
>
> "I live in a borough."
>
> "Is a borough a kind of municipality?"
>
> "Yes."
>
> "Thank you. Got it."

1.2. Benefits of Transparency

Transparency promotes understanding. We are increasingly relying on computers for advice. When a computer is transparent about how it produced a recommendation, we understand it better. This allows us to make an informed decision about whether to accept it.

> The computer says, "I recommend that you call Nikita Deshaun to pitch yourself for the role of Judge in a sports drink commercial she is currently casting."
>
> "Why?" asks Keith.
>
> "Because you have a headshot in which you portray a judge, and she has called you in before."

Transparency is educational. Transparent computers can help us learn new things.

> "Enoxaparin is recommended to reduce coagulation," says the computer.
>
> "How does Enoxaparin reduce coagulation?" asks Christopher.
>
> "Enoxaparin increases antithrombin, which inactivates clotting factor Xa, which is pivotal to coagulation."

Transparency makes it easier to fix problems. When a problem occurs and the computer is transparent about it, we get a better understanding of it. This allows us to recover from it more easily.

> "Why is my clock seven minutes fast?" says Alexis.
>
> "The clock is set to manual and running exclusively on an internal crystal oscillator," responds the phone. "Shall I set the clock to automatic so that it regularly updates the time from the network?"
>
> "Yes, please."

Transparency improves customer satisfaction. Computers can be very frustrating. When a computer is transparent, our frustration is reduced, and we are happier.

"Your payment has been received, and your available credit has been increased. Shall I order your medium pizza with mushrooms now?"

"Yes," says Jessica.

"Done."

"Awesome!"

Transparency builds trust. As we become more familiar with a computer's internals, our trust in the computer increases.

1.3. Creating Transparent Computers

In this book, I describe techniques for designing and building transparent computers. I draw heavily on techniques that have been developed in the field of artificial intelligence, because transparent computers require a degree of intelligence. (The term "transparent" is sometimes used to describe systems whose internals are invisible. By transparent, I mean the opposite—that the system's internals are visible.)

Part I presents methods useful for designing and building transparent computers. Chapter 2 discusses declarative methods, chapter 3 discusses computer programs, and chapter 4 discusses neural networks. Part II describes in more detail how to implement the key aspects of transparent computers. Chapter 5 discusses dialogue, chapter 6 discusses explanation, and chapter 7 discusses learning. Chapter 8 presents my conclusion.

1.4. Summary

Computers should be transparent, not opaque. Their operation should be understandable to people. They should be able to reason like people, explain their reasoning, engage in dialogues, and learn through interaction. It's important for computers to be transparent, because transparency promotes understanding, is educational, makes it easier to fix problems, improves customer satisfaction, and builds trust.

Part I.

Methods for Transparency

2. Declarative Methods for Transparency

In standard programming, we write computer programs that tell the computer what to do. For example, we tell it to execute statement S_1, followed by S_2, followed by S_3. In contrast, with *declarative methods*, we describe a problem—typically using logical formulas or mathematical expressions—and then we let the computer figure out what to do to solve it. For example, we feed a set of simultaneous equations to a *solver* that solves them. In this chapter, I discuss several declarative methods useful for creating transparent computers: satisfiability, deduction, default reasoning, answer set programming, and dependencies.

2.1. Satisfiability

One basic declarative method is *satisfiability*. Suppose we are given the following *constraints* about propositions p, q, and r:

$p \lor q$
$q \lor \lnot r$
$r \lor \lnot p$

($\lor$ means "or" and $\lnot$ means "not.") What truth assignments of p, q, and r satisfy these constraints? This is called a *satisfiability problem*, and it has three solutions or *models*:

1. $\lnot p, q, r$ (This means that p is false, q is true, and r is true.)

2. $\lnot p, q, \lnot r$

3. p, q, r

Satisfiability problems can be solved using *satisfiability solvers*. A simple way of solving these problems is exhaustive search. For each possible truth assignment, we check whether or not the truth assignment satisfies the constraints. For example, the truth assignment

$$p, q, r$$

satisfies all the constraints, so it is a solution to the problem. On the other hand, the truth assignment

$$p, q, \neg r$$

violates the constraint

$$r \vee \neg p$$

so it is not a solution to the problem. In practice, more efficient methods are used to search the space of truth assignments.

How understandable are models? Can they serve as explanations? Models themselves are highly understandable. Each model provides a concrete example of what is possible given the constraints. It's also easy to see why a given truth assignment is not a model, because we only have to notice that it violates a single constraint. For example, $p, q, \neg r$ is not a model because it violates the one constraint $r \vee \neg p$.

On the other hand, it's more difficult to see why a truth assignment is a model, because we have to verify that the truth assignment satisfies all the constraints.

What if we want an explanation of why a particular proposition is true or false? For this, it's more convenient to use deduction.

2.2. Deduction

We start with sets of *inference rules* and *logical axioms*. One inference rule is *modus ponens*:

Infer B from A and $A \rightarrow B$.

($\rightarrow$ means "implies.")

Another one is *conjunction*:

Infer $A \wedge B$ from A and B.

($\wedge$ means "and.") An example of a logical axiom is

$q \rightarrow (p \rightarrow q)$

A *deduction* or *proof* of a formula Y from a set of formulas X is a sequence of formulas, where the last formula is Y, and each formula in the sequence is either

- a logical axiom,

- a formula in X, or

- a formula inferred from previous formulas using an inference rule.

For example, suppose X is the following:

p
q
$p \wedge q \rightarrow r$
$r \rightarrow s$

Here is a deduction of s from X:

1. p

2. q

3. $p \wedge q$ (from 1 and 2 using conjunction)

4. $p \wedge q \rightarrow r$

5. r (from 3 and 4 using modus ponens)

6. $r \rightarrow s$

7. s (from 5 and 6 using modus ponens)

Proofs can be generated automatically by automated theorem proving programs. Provided that they aren't too complicated, proofs make good explanations, because they are instances of valid reasoning.

2.3. Default Reasoning

Because the world is full of exceptions, we can't always describe it using simple formulas of the form

$$p \rightarrow q$$

We have to include exceptions in our formulas:

$$p \wedge \neg e \rightarrow q$$

For example, p might be "the light is turned on," q might be "the light goes on," and e might be "the light is broken." It would be nice if we could assume that e is false by *default*. That is, unless we are explicitly told that the light is broken, we assume that it is not.

2.4. Answer Set Programming

The technique of *answer set programming* supports reasoning by default. The previous formula is expressed in answer set programming as follows:

```
q :- p, not e.
```

This is called a *rule*. The *head* of the rule is q, and the *body* of the rule is p, not e. An example of a *fact* is the following:

```
p.
```

A set of rules and facts is called an *answer set program*.
   If we feed the answer set program

```
q :- p, not e.
p.
```

to an *answer set solver*, then it will produce the following *answer set*:

```
p q
```

This means that p and q are true. Because e is false by default, the rule applies and q is true.

If, however, we feed

```
q :- p, not e.
p.
e.
```

to the solver, then it will produce the answer set

```
p e
```

Because e is true, the rule no longer applies, and q is no longer true.

Answer Set Programming Versus Satisfiability

Answer set programming differs in an important way from satisfiability. Suppose we are given the following constraints:

$$p$$
$$p \wedge \neg e \rightarrow q$$

Instead of producing one answer set, a satisfiability solver produces three models:

1. $p, q, \neg e$

2. $p, \neg q, e$

3. p, q, e

Answer set programming assumes that a proposition like e is false in an answer set unless a rule justifies it in the answer set. Satisfiability doesn't make any such assumption. Instead, satisfiability gives us all the truth assignments that satisfy the constraints.

2.5. Dependencies

A *dependency* specifies that one variable is a function of one or more other variables. For example, we may specify that x is the sum of y and z:

```
x:y+z
```

If we change y or z, then x will be *marked invalid*, and x will be recomputed from y and z the next time it is referenced or displayed. Suppose we further specify that y is the sum of a and b:

    y : a+b

Then, if we change a, both y and x will be marked invalid.

Dependencies support transparency. If we want to understand how x is computed, then we can look at its definition. If we are further curious about y, then we can look at its definition. We can create a user interface that allows us to view a variable's definition by clicking on it.

Spreadsheets

Dependencies are used in spreadsheets. We can type a formula into a cell that contains references to other cells. If we type a new value into a cell, then all cells that depend on that cell are immediately recomputed.

Tax Preparation Systems

Dependencies are used in income tax preparation systems. We answer questions and enter our financial data into worksheets. Calculations are performed on the data, and the results are transferred to our tax forms. We can click on a cell in a form to find out how its value was calculated.

2.6. Summary

We can build transparent systems using declarative methods. These include satisfiability, automated deduction, default reasoning, answer set programming, and dependencies. Satisfiability provides explanations in the form of models, whereas automated deduction provides explanations in the form of proofs. We may use one or more of these methods depending on the application.

2.7. Further Reading

Gomes, Kautz, Sabharwal, and Selman (2008) discuss satisfiability. Mendelson (2015) discusses deduction. Robinson and Voronkov (2001) discuss automated theorem proving. Brewka, Niemelä, and Truszczyński (2008) discuss default reasoning. Mueller (2015) discusses default reasoning about action and change. Gebser, Kaminski, Kaufmann, and Schaub (2013) provide a practical guide to answer set programming. Dependencies are implemented in the A+ array-oriented programming language (`http://www.aplusdev.org`), which is a variant of APL. Johnson-Laird (1983) discusses human reasoning using models, and Rips (1994) discusses human reasoning using proofs.

3. Transparent Computer Programs

Computer programs tend to be complicated. How can we make them more transparent and understandable to programmers and end users? In this chapter, I discuss several approaches to this problem, including decomposition, functional programming, specification, and interactive programming environments.

3.1. Decomposition

One way of making computer programs more understandable is to decompose them into small procedures that make sense to people. Suppose we're writing a Python program that decides whether to decline a customer's credit card transaction. We might be tempted to write a single procedure to do this. But we notice that the customer's available credit is a meaningful concept in banking. Therefore, we break the problem into two small procedures:

```python
def declined(t):
  return t.amount > availableCredit(t.customer)

def availableCredit(c):
  return c.totalCreditLimit - c.balance - c.pending
```

The variable t refers to a financial transaction, and c refers to a customer. We can create a user interface that allows us to see what procedures were used to compute a given value.

3.2. Functional Programming

Another way of making computer programs more understandable is to use *functional programming*. In this style of programming, we write procedures that implement mathematical *functions* that associate each input with a unique output. We attempt to avoid or eliminate procedures with *side effects* like modification of global variables or inputs.

Procedures with side effects can be more difficult to understand than procedures without side effects. Consider the following Python procedure f, which modifies the global variable V and whose output depends on V:

```python
def f(x):
  global V
  V=V+1
  return x*V
```

What is the value of the expression f(10)? Its value depends on the initial value of the global variable V. If V is 0, then f(10) is 10, whereas, if V is 1, then f(10) is 20. This may be confusing.

Furthermore, suppose that V is initialized to 0. Then the value of f(10)+f(20) is 50, whereas the value of f(20)+f(10) is 40. This seems strange, because addition is commutative. (The procedure f is the culprit here, not addition.)

3.3. Specification

Another way of making computer programs more understandable is to add *specifications* to procedures. A procedure's *precondition* specifies what is true before the procedure is executed, and its *postcondition* specifies what is true after it is executed.

Informal Specifications

We write *informal specifications* in a natural language like English.

In Python, we can write informal specifications using comments or docstrings:

```python
def sqrt(x):
    """Returns the square root of x."""
    return pow(x,0.5)
```

Formal Specifications

We write *formal specifications* using logical or other formal languages. In Python, we can write formal specifications using the contract package:

```python
import contract
import numpy

def sqrt(x):
    """
    pre:
        x>=0
    post:
        numpy.isclose(__return__*__return__,x)
    """
    return pow(x,0.5)

contract.checkmod(__name__)
```

The pre specification states that the input x is greater than or equal to zero. The post specification states that the square of the output is approximately equal to x.

Violations of formal specifications can be detected when running a program. An error message will be produced if a precondition or postcondition is violated.

Verification

In some cases, we can use formal specifications to prove general results about a procedure that are independent of particular inputs.

19

We may be able to prove or *verify* that, if the precondition is true before executing the procedure, and the procedure terminates, then the postcondition is true after executing the procedure. This is called a *program correctness proof*.

3.4. Interactive Programming Environments

A number of features can be added to interactive programming environments to make computer programs more transparent.

Execution Highlighting

Statements that have been executed since the last interaction can be highlighted. This allows the programmer or end user to understand what parts of the program were involved in processing the interaction.

Reversible Execution

Computer programs normally run forward, but they can be made reversible. A program can be run in reverse to find out what statement was responsible for modifying a given variable or field of a data structure. This is particularly useful for tracking down a problem when the value of the variable or field appears to be incorrect. The program can be further run in reverse to see the previous value of the variable or field.

3.5. Summary

Computer programs can be made more transparent by decomposing programs into small procedures and by using functional programming, specifications, and programming environments that support execution highlighting and reversible execution.

3.6. Further Reading

Lampson (1983) provides hints for computer system design. Liskov and Guttag (2001) discuss specification, and Hoare (1969) discusses program correctness proofs. Archer, Conway, and Schneider (1984) discuss reversible programs. The ability to run programs in forward or reverse improves the user's experience of *immediacy*, as discussed by Ungar, Lieberman, and Fry (1997).

4. Neural Networks for Transparency

Inspired by the physiology of the brain, *neural networks* are large networks of simple processing units. They are capable of approximating any continuous function and can be used for a variety of tasks. Neural networks have been developed to identify and locate objects in images, convert speech or handwriting into text, predict the next word of a sentence, and translate sentences from one language to another. In this chapter, I present the basics of neural networks, and then I discuss approaches for supporting transparency using neural networks.

4.1. Sigmoid Units

A neural network consists of many *units* connected together. A typical unit, called a *sigmoid unit*, computes the sum of its inputs $x_1, \ldots, x_n$ weighted by *weights* $w_1, \ldots, w_n$, applies the sigmoid function, and feeds the result to its output or *activation* y:

$$y = \frac{1}{1 + e^{-\sum_{i=1}^{n} w_i x_i}}$$

4.2. Feedforward Networks

A typical *feedforward network* consists of a sequence of *layers* of units. There is an input layer, followed by one or more hidden layers, followed by an output layer. A feedforward network with one hidden layer is shown in figure 4.1. The units in the input layer are not full

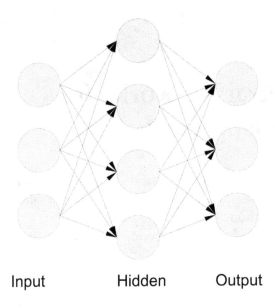

Input   Hidden   Output

Figure 4.1. Feedforward network with one hidden layer

sigmoid units but rather simply feed into the first hidden layer. The units in each hidden layer feed into the next layer.

4.3. Training Neural Networks

We can get a neural network to compute a given function or perform a given task by setting the weights of the units appropriately. The process of determining values for these weights is called *training*. We start by obtaining or creating a set of *training examples* for the function or task of interest. Each training example consists of the inputs to the network and the desired outputs of the network—what we would like the outputs of the network to be given those inputs.

Backpropagation

One training algorithm that is commonly used is *backpropagation*:

1. Set the network's weights to small random values.

2. Until a stopping condition is reached, do the following:

   - For each training example, do the following:

     a) Propagate the input forward:

        - Feed the input from the training example into the network and compute the outputs of all the units in the network.

     b) Propagate the errors backward:

        - Compute the error of each output unit by comparing the unit's output with the desired output from the training example.

        - Compute the error of each hidden unit from the errors of the units in the following layer.

     c) Adjust the weights to reduce the errors.

4.4. Reasoning with Neural Networks

Typically, we feed an input into a neural network, such as an image of an animal, and it produces an output, like a classification of the animal's species. Is this reasoning?

The 1828 edition of *Webster's Revised Unabridged Dictionary*, available at `http://machaut.uchicago.edu/websters`, defines reasoning as follows:

> RE"ASONING, ppr. arguing; deducing inferences from premises; debating; discussing.
>
> RE"ASONING, n. The act or process of exercising the faculty of reason; that act or operation of the mind by which new or unknown propositions are deduced from previous ones which are known and evident, or which

are admitted or supposed for the sake of argument; argumentation; ratiocination; as fair reasoning; false reasoning; absurd reasoning; strong or weak reasoning. The reasonings of the advocate appeared to the court conclusive.

The typical neural network doesn't seem to be doing this. At most, it seems to be doing a single step of reasoning. The question is, How can we use neural networks for reasoning, especially reasoning involving multiple steps?

Tic-Tac-Toe

David Rumelhart, Paul Smolensky, James McClelland, and Geoffrey Hinton demonstrated a simple form of multi-step reasoning using neural networks. They connected two networks together to play a game of tic-tac-toe. One network would make a move, and the other network would respond, until the game was over.

Recurrent Neural Networks

Another approach to the problem of multi-step reasoning is to use *recurrent neural networks*. A recurrent neural network maintains memory across multiple *time steps*. We add units to the network to serve as memory, and we update the activations of these units at time step t based on

- the activations of these units at time step $t - 1$,

- the output of the network at time step $t - 1$, and

- the inputs to the network at time step t.

Several researchers have demonstrated the use of recurrent neural networks to perform multiple steps of deduction.

4.5. Understanding Neural Networks

A neural network contains lots of weights, and when we feed an input into a neural network, we compute lots of activations. The trouble is that it's difficult to understand these weights and activations. How do we make neural networks more understandable?

Rule Extraction

One approach to understanding neural networks is to extract rules from them. We feed input examples into a trained neural network, and we record the corresponding outputs. The examples can be training examples, randomly generated examples, or other examples. We then use algorithms like ID3 or Prism to generate decision trees or rules from the inputs to the network and the corresponding outputs. Before using the extracted rules, we can evaluate the degree to which they match the neural network on a set of test examples.

Data Visualization

Another approach to understanding neural networks is to use data visualization techniques. For example, we can display weights and activations with different colors or gray levels. *Hinton diagrams* display positive weights as white rectangles and negative weights as black rectangles. The magnitude of the weight is indicated by the size of the rectangle. For neural networks that classify images, we can visualize the network's notion of a given class—like *Dalmatian* or *cup*—by finding an input image that produces a high score for that class. For a specific image, we can also highlight the parts of an image that are the most salient for a given class. We can also use techniques like principal component analysis to reduce the dimensionality of the data.

4.6. Neural Network Architectures

We can design larger architectures for reasoning that use neural networks as building blocks. Each neural network, for example, can perform a single step of reasoning. Then, to perform n steps of reasoning, we use n networks and feed the output of each network into the input of the next one.

4.7. Neural Networks with Explanation

We can create neural networks that are specially designed to support explanation. We can train them to produce explanations along with their conclusions. The explanations are provided on an additional set of output nodes.

4.8. Summary

Neural networks are large networks of simple processing units, often organized into layers. The units compute a weighted sum of their inputs, and the weights are trained from examples. Neural networks typically perform a single step of reasoning. Nevertheless, by connecting multiple neural networks together—or by feeding their output back into their input—they can perform multiple steps of reasoning. Neural networks can be hard to understand because they consist of many numbers. They can be made more understandable by extracting rules from them and using data visualization techniques. It should be possible to extend neural networks with more reasoning and explanation capabilities.

4.9. Further Reading

Neural Networks

Mitchell (1997) discusses a variety of machine learning techniques including neural networks. LeCun, Bengio, and Hinton (2015) discuss *deep neural networks*.

Tic-Tac-Toe

Rumelhart, Smolensky, McClelland, and Hinton (1986) connected together two neural networks to play tic-tac-toe. Michie (1974) implemented a tic-tac-toe program based on reinforcement learning in which "a mechanical Nought plays against a mechanical Cross" (p. 17). Babbage (1864, pp. 465–470) sketched out a mechanism for playing tic-tac-toe.

Reasoning

Bader, Hitzler, and Hölldobler (2008) describe a recurrent neural network that performs deduction. Weston et al. (2015) use *memory networks* to address the bAbI tasks, which involve answering questions about simple stories. Yang, He, Gao, Deng, and Smola (2015) use *stacked attention networks* to perform multiple reasoning steps to answer questions about images like *What's sitting in the basket on the bicycle?* The Workshop on Neural-Symbolic Learning and Reasoning (`http://www.neural-symbolic.org`) focuses on the use of neural networks for reasoning.

Rule Extraction

Andrews, Diederich, and Tickle (1995) review methods for extracting rules from neural networks. Craven and Shavlik (1996) and Baesens, Setiono, Mues, and Vanthienen (2003) evaluate several such methods. Quinlan (1986) discusses the ID3 decision tree induction algorithm, and Cendrowska (1987) discusses the Prism rule induction algorithm.

Data Visualization

Tufte (2001) discusses data visualization. Hinton and Sejnowski (1986, p. 301) discuss Hinton diagrams. Simonyan, Vedaldi, and Zisserman (2014) discuss visualization of classes in deep convolutional networks. Dennis and Phillips (1991) discuss using principal component analysis to analyze hidden unit activations.

Part II.

Aspects of Transparency

5. Dialogue

Dialogue is essential for transparent computers. We should be able to make requests and clarify them through dialogue. We should be able to dig into what we don't understand through dialogue—by asking questions and getting answers. Dialogue is useful for accomplishing many types of tasks, including diagnosing and fixing problems, finding products, placing orders, signing up for events, setting up meetings, and conducting surveys. In this chapter, I describe several types of dialogue, and then I discuss techniques for implementing dialogue.

5.1. Reactive Dialogue

Several types of dialogue can be implemented. In *reactive dialogue*, the system simply reacts to incoming requests or questions and may have little or no memory of the previous dialogue. For example:

> Xavier says, "Please order me another box of paper for my printer."
>
> The computer responds, "Done."

5.2. Goal-Based Dialogue

In *goal-based dialogue*, the system carries out a dialogue on behalf of a particular goal. The goal may be the user's goal, such as the goal to book a vacation. Or the goal may be the system's goal, such as the goal to elicit information from the user.

5.3. Clarification Dialogue

A *clarification dialogue* is used when the system doesn't have enough information to complete a request. For example, the request may be ambiguous:

> Xavier asks, "What's the weather in Portland?"
>
> "Do you mean Portland, Oregon or Portland, Maine?"
>
> "Portland, Oregon."
>
> "It's 42 degrees and cloudy, with a 52 percent chance of precipitation."

The original request may not be spelled out in enough detail:

> Melanie says, "Book me a trip to New York leaving Monday morning and returning Thursday evening."
>
> "Would you like me to book your favorite hotel?"
>
> "Yes, please."
>
> "Done. I have booked your train and hotel."

5.4. Dialogue Manager

To implement dialogues, we create a *dialogue manager* that manages communication with the user. The dialogue manager receives input from the user and sends output back to the user. It can communicate with the user via text, speech, images, or video. It typically connects to services like question answering services, transaction services, and databases.

The dialogue manager maintains information about the state of the dialogue and the user. Depending on the situation or application, the dialogue manager can implement reactive dialogues, goal-based dialogues, or clarification dialogues.

5.5. Planning for Dialogues

The most general technique for generating dialogues is to use *automated planning*—generating a sequence of actions for achieving a goal. We run a *planner* after each utterance, to determine the best dialogue and external actions to perform.

5.6. Transition Networks

Another technique for generating dialogues is to use *transition networks*. A transition network consists of

- a set of *states* and

- a set of *transitions* between the states.

A transition consists of

- the user's utterance,

- the system's response to the user's utterance, and

- the next state.

The system's response can be utterances or other actions.

5.7. Implementing a Dialogue

We can implement a dialogue in Python using transition networks. We use one *state procedure* for each state of the transition network. As input, the state procedure takes a user's utterance and a data structure that holds additional data such as information gathered from the user. As output, the state procedure returns a pair consisting of

- the system's utterance to send to the user and

- the next state, which is another procedure.

If the next state is None, then the dialogue terminates. If the state procedure returns None instead of a pair, then the system repeats its previous utterance and stays in the same state.

Implementing the State Procedures

For example, we can implement a dialogue for signing up for a dance class as follows. The first state is the `start` state:

```
def start(s,d):
    if re.search(r'\b(want|would like)\b.*\bdance\b',s):
        return ('Beginner, intermediate, or advanced?',level)
    return None
```

When the user wants to sign up for a class, the system asks the user for the desired level of class, and the system transitions to the `level` state:

```
def level(s,d):
    m=re.search(r'\b(beginner|intermediate|advanced)\b',s)
    if not m: return None
    d['level']=m.group(1)
    return ('What style of dance?',style)
```

After the user specifies the desired level of class, the system asks the user for the style of dance, and the system transitions to the `style` state:

```
def style(s,d):
    m=re.search(r'\b(ballet|jazz|modern|hip hop)\b',s)
    if not m:
        return ('We have ballet, jazz, modern, and '+
                'hip hop. Which would you like?',style)
    d['style']=m.group(1)
    return ('Afternoon or evening?',timeOfDay)
```

If the user doesn't specify one of the available styles of dance, the system tells the user what styles are available, and it continues in the same state. Otherwise, the system asks for the desired time of day of the class, and it transitions to the `timeOfDay` state:

```
def timeOfDay(s,d):
    m=re.search(r'\b(afternoon|evening)\b',s)
```

```
if not m: return None
d['timeOfDay']=m.group(1)
d['class']=suggestClass(d)
return ('Shall I sign you up for '+d['class']+'?',book)
```

After the user specifies the desired time of day, the system finds a class that meets the user's criteria, it asks whether the user wishes to sign up for the class, and it transitions to the book state:

```
def book(s,d):
  m=re.search(r'\b(yes|no)\b',s)
  if not m: return None
  if m.group(1)=='yes':
    d['confirm']=bookClass(d)
    return ('Your confirmation number is '+
            d['confirm']+'.',None)
  return ('OK, thank you anyway.',None)
```

If the user says yes, then the system books the class, it responds with a confirmation number, and the dialogue terminates.

Running the Dialogue

The state procedures can be tested using a top-level loop like the following:

```
def dm():
  d={}
  state=start
  s1=None
  while state:
    if s1: print(s1)
    print('> ',end='')
    s=input().lower()
    t=state(s,d)
    if t: (s1,state)=t
  print(s1)
  print(d)
```

Here is a dialogue supported by the previous procedures:

```
> I want to take a dance class.
Beginner, intermediate, or advanced?
> intermediate please
What style of dance?
> Flamenco
We have ballet, jazz, modern, and hip hop. Which would
you like?
> Hip hop
Afternoon or evening?
> evening
Shall I sign you up for Intermediate Hip Hop Friday at
7 PM?
> yes
Your confirmation number is 3552.
{'timeOfDay': 'evening',
 'confirm': '3552',
 'style': 'hip hop',
 'class': 'Intermediate Hip Hop Friday at 7 PM',
 'level': 'intermediate'}
```

5.8. Summary

Transparent computers should be able to engage in dialogues. Types of dialogue include reactive dialogue, goal-based dialogue, and clarification dialogue. Dialogues with the user can be managed by a dialogue manager, which communicates with the user and connects to other services. Dialogues can be implemented using automated planning or transition networks.

5.9. Further Reading

Green (1986) discusses the use of transition networks for dialogue. Jokinen and McTear (2010) discuss spoken dialogue systems. Ghallab, Nau, and Traverso (2004) discuss automated planning.

6. Explanation

Explanation is key to transparency. When a computer generates a conclusion or performs an action, it should be able to explain—in terms the user can understand—how it generated the conclusion or why it performed the action. In this chapter, I discuss types of explanation requests, and I describe how explanation can be implemented.

6.1. Explanation Requests

Instead of providing explanations all the time, the system typically provides them in response to an *explanation request*. Some explanation requests are as simple as *why?* or *why not?* Other explanation requests are of the form *why X?* or *why not X?*, where X is a conclusion, action, diagnosis, recommendation, or goal. A user can also ask the system why it asked a given question.

6.2. Implementing Explanation

How do we explain the system's internal processes to the user? If the system is using deduction, then we can present deductions to the user. If it is using satisfiability, then we can present models to the user. If it is written using a standard computer program, then we can highlight the statements that were executed.

Let's consider how to generate explanations when the system is using answer set programming. We use the example of deciding whether to accept or reject a customer's credit card transaction.

Rules

We create some rules for making the decision:

```
declined(TID) :-
  amount(TID,AMOUNT),
  customer(TID,CID),
  availableCredit(CID,CREDIT),
  AMOUNT>CREDIT.

availableCredit(CID,CREDIT) :-
  totalCreditLimit(CID,LIMIT),
  currentBalance(CID,BALANCE),
  pendingCharges(CID,PENDING),
  CREDIT=LIMIT-BALANCE-PENDING.
```

These rules contain the following variables:

- TID: the transaction ID

- CID: the customer ID

- AMOUNT: the transaction amount

- BALANCE: the customer's current balance

- CREDIT: the customer's available credit

- LIMIT: the customer's total credit limit

- PENDING: the customer's pending charges

Natural Language Mappings

To support generation of these rules in natural language, we create some natural language mappings:

```
declined(TID) ->
  your transaction is declined
```

```
amount(TID,AMOUNT) ->
  the transaction amount is AMOUNT

availableCredit(CID,CREDIT) ->
  your available credit is CREDIT

totalCreditLimit(CID,LIMIT) ->
  your total credit limit is LIMIT

currentBalance(CID,BALANCE) ->
  your current balance is BALANCE

pendingCharges(CID,PENDING) ->
  you have PENDING in pending charges
```

Explanation Generator

We build an explanation generator. As input, it takes the following:

- a set of rules,

- a set of natural language mappings,

- an answer set from the answer set solver, and

- a proposition to be explained.

As output, it produces a natural language explanation.

The explanation generator first locates a rule that justifies the proposition to be explained with respect to the answer set. It then uses the natural language mappings to generate the head of the rule, followed by the word *because*, followed by the body of the rule. Propositions without a natural language mapping, like customer(tid1,cid1), are omitted. Appropriate capitalization, punctuation, and conjunctions are produced.

Suppose the proposition to be explained is `declined(tid1)` and the answer set is

```
amount(tid1,1175)
customer(tid1,cid1)
totalCreditLimit(cid1,500000)
currentBalance(cid1,483849)
pendingCharges(cid1,15427)
availableCredit(cid1,724)
declined(tid1)
```

(Amounts are in cents.)

Then the following rule justifies `declined(tid1)`:

```
declined(tid1) :- amount(tid1,1175),
    customer(tid1,cid1),
    availableCredit(cid1,724),
    1175>724.
```

The following explanation is produced:

> Your transaction is declined because the transaction amount is 1175, and your available credit is 724.

6.3. Explanation and Dialogue

A problem with using rules directly for explanation is that the rules may not be at the right level of detail for the user. They may be too detailed, or they may not be detailed enough. The user should be able to control the level of detail through dialogue.

Here's an example of how the user can get a more detailed explanation. The previous explanation was generated from the rule that rejected the credit card transaction. That rule made use of the available credit, which was determined by another rule. If the user wants an explanation of the available credit, then the user can ask for it.

The system responds with the following:

> Your available credit is 724 because your total credit limit is 500000, your current balance is 483849, and you have 15427 in pending charges.

But suppose the user questions the very rule that the transaction is declined when the amount is greater than the available credit. One way to address this is to create more detailed rules.

6.4. Summary

A transparent computer should be able to explain the results it produces. The declarative method of deduction produces explanations as part of its normal operation. To generate explanations of conclusions generated using answer set programming, we convert rules that led to those conclusions into natural language. Getting the right level of detail in an explanation may require dialogue.

6.5. Further Reading

Scott, Clancey, Davis, and Shortliffe (1984) and Wieland (1990) discuss methods for generating explanations from rules. Reiter and Dale (2000) discuss natural language generation. Stent and Bangalore (2014) discuss natural language generation as it relates to interactive systems. Moore (1995) discusses the need for dialogue in explanation.

7. Learning

A transparent computer should be able to learn from the user, and what it has learned should be transparent. When a piece of knowledge is incorrect, the user should be able to correct it. By interacting with the user, the computer's knowledge will improve over time. In this chapter, I discuss three techniques for learning from the user: decision tree induction, active learning, and synonym learning.

7.1. Decision Tree Induction

A system can generate decision trees using *decision tree induction* algorithms like ID3. Here's an example using ID3 in Weka (http://www.cs.waikato.ac.nz/ml/weka/). The system collects some initial examples of the user's activities on various days, and it runs ID3 on them:

```
@RELATION activity
@ATTRIBUTE weekday {n,y}
@ATTRIBUTE holiday {n,y}
@ATTRIBUTE summer {n,y}
@ATTRIBUTE class {teach,work,relax}

@DATA
y,n,n,teach
y,n,y,work
y,y,n,relax
n,n,n,relax
```

The first example is that, on a day that is a weekday, not a holiday, and not in the summer, the user is teaching.

Given these examples, ID3 produces the following decision tree:

```
summer = n
|   weekday = n: relax
|   weekday = y
|   |   holiday = n: teach
|   |   holiday = y: relax
summer = y: work
```

Now suppose that it's a weekend in the summer. The system predicts that the user is working, but the user is actually relaxing. The user asks the system for an explanation. Based on the decision tree, its explanation is that, if it's summer, then you're working. The user informs the system that this is incorrect—the user is in fact relaxing.

The system adds the following example:

```
n,n,y,relax
```

It reruns ID3, which produces this new decision tree:

```
weekday = n: relax
weekday = y
|   holiday = n
|   |   summer = n: teach
|   |   summer = y: work
|   holiday = y: relax
```

The system's knowledge is transparent, and this knowledge can be modified by the user.

7.2. Active Learning

In the previous example, the user noticed a problem with the system's knowledge. In *active learning*, the system actively seeks knowledge. Several techniques have been developed for finding and closing knowledge gaps.

The Learner system starts with existing knowledge and generates hypotheses to be confirmed or refuted by the user. For example:

> "Dogs purr when stroked?" asks the computer.
>
> "No, they don't," says the user.
>
> "OK."

7.3. Synonym Learning

One of the things that makes natural language so difficult for computers is that there are so many ways of saying the same thing. In medicine, for example, a given drug can have many names. Synonyms for *aspirin* include the following:

> acetylsalicylic acid
> ASA
> 2-acetyloxybenzoic acid
> Ecotrin
> Empirin
> Entericin
> Extren
> Measurin

A transparent system should allow the user to add synonyms to its *lexical database* for future use:

> "I took an Aspergum," says the user.
>
> "What is an Aspergum?" the computer replies. "Aspirin was recommended."
>
> "Aspergum is the same as aspirin."
>
> "OK. Understood."

7.4. Summary

Transparent computers should learn through interaction. A computer's knowledge should be transparent to users, and users should be able to modify the computer's knowledge when necessary. Some techniques for learning from the user include decision tree induction, active learning, and synonym learning.

7.5. Further Reading

Mitchell (1997) discusses machine learning techniques, and Quinlan (1986) discusses the ID3 algorithm. Chklovski (2003) describes the Learner system. Jurafsky and Martin (2009) discuss natural language processing, and Fellbaum (1998) discusses the WordNet lexical database.

8. Conclusion

It's essential for computers to be transparent as they become more integrated into all aspects of life. To be transparent, computers should reason like people, should be able to explain their reasoning to people, should be able to have dialogues with people, and should learn by interacting with people. Many techniques exist for supporting transparency, and we can use them right now to design and build transparent computers.

Acknowledgments

I thank my teachers, colleagues, friends, and family for teaching me about computers and artificial intelligence and for helping me develop these ideas. Special thanks to Susanna and Matt.

References

Andrews, R., Diederich, J., & Tickle, A. B. (1995). Survey and critique of techniques for extracting rules from trained artificial neural networks. *Knowledge-Based Systems, 8*(6), 373–389.

Archer, Jr., J. E., Conway, R., & Schneider, F. B. (1984). User recovery and reversal in interactive systems. *ACM Transactions on Programming Languages and Systems, 6*(1), 1–19.

Babbage, C. (1864). *Passages from the life of a philosopher*. London: Longman, Green, Longman, Roberts, & Green.

Bader, S., Hitzler, P., & Hölldobler, S. (2008). Connectionist model generation: A first-order approach. *Neurocomputing, 71*(13–15), 2420–2432.

Baesens, B., Setiono, R., Mues, C., & Vanthienen, J. (2003). Using neural network rule extraction and decision tables for credit-risk evaluation. *Management Science, 49*(3), 312–329.

Brewka, G., Niemelä, I., & Truszczyński, M. (2008). Nonmonotonic reasoning. In F. van Harmelen, V. Lifschitz, & B. Porter (Eds.), *Handbook of knowledge representation* (pp. 239–284). Amsterdam: Elsevier.

Cendrowska, J. (1987). PRISM: An algorithm for inducing modular rules. *International Journal of Man-Machine Studies, 27*(4), 349–370.

Chklovski, T. (2003). *Using analogy to acquire commonsense knowledge from human contributors* (Tech. Rep. No. AITR-2003-002). Cambridge, MA: Artificial Intelligence Laboratory, Massachusetts Institute of Technology.

Craven, M., & Shavlik, J. W. (1996). Extracting tree-structured representations of trained networks. In D. S. Touretzky, M. C. Mozer, & M. E. Hasselmo (Eds.), *Advances in neural information processing systems 8* (pp. 24–30). Cambridge, MA: MIT Press.

Dennis, S., & Phillips, S. (1991). *Analysis tools for neural networks* (Tech. Rep. No. 207). Queensland, Australia: Department of Computer Science, University of Queensland.

Fellbaum, C. (Ed.). (1998). *WordNet: An electronic lexical database.* Cambridge, MA: MIT Press.

Gebser, M., Kaminski, R., Kaufmann, B., & Schaub, T. (2013). *Answer set solving in practice.* San Rafael, CA: Morgan & Claypool.

Ghallab, M., Nau, D., & Traverso, P. (2004). *Automated planning: Theory and practice.* San Francisco: Morgan Kaufmann.

Gomes, C. P., Kautz, H., Sabharwal, A., & Selman, B. (2008). Satisfiability solvers. In F. van Harmelen, V. Lifschitz, & B. Porter (Eds.), *Handbook of knowledge representation* (pp. 89–134). Amsterdam: Elsevier.

Green, M. (1986). A survey of three dialogue models. *ACM Transactions on Graphics, 5*(3), 244–275.

Hinton, G. E., & Sejnowski, T. J. (1986). Learning and relearning in Boltzmann machines. In D. E. Rumelhart, J. L. McClelland, & PDP Research Group (Eds.), *Parallel distributed processing: Explorations in the microstructure of cognition* (Vol. 1: Foundations, pp. 282–317). Cambridge, MA: MIT Press.

Hoare, C. A. R. (1969). An axiomatic basis for computer programming. *Communications of the ACM, 12*(10), 576–583.

Johnson-Laird, P. N. (1983). *Mental models: Toward a cognitive science of language, inference, and consciousness.* Cambridge, MA: Harvard University Press.

Jokinen, K., & McTear, M. (2010). *Spoken dialogue systems.* San Rafael, CA: Morgan & Claypool.

Jurafsky, D., & Martin, J. H. (2009). *Speech and language processing: An introduction to natural language processing, computational linguistics, and speech recognition* (Second ed.). Upper Saddle River, NJ: Prentice Hall.

Lampson, B. W. (1983). Hints for computer system design. *Operating Systems Review, 17*(5), 33–48.

LeCun, Y., Bengio, Y., & Hinton, G. E. (2015). Deep learning. *Nature, 521,* 436–444.

Liskov, B., & Guttag, J. (2001). *Program development in Java: Abstrac-*

tion, specification, and object-oriented design. Boston: Addison-Wesley.

Mendelson, E. (2015). *Introduction to mathematical logic* (Sixth ed.). Boca Raton, FL: CRC Press.

Michie, D. (1974). *On machine intelligence*. New York: John Wiley.

Mitchell, T. M. (1997). *Machine learning*. Boston: McGraw-Hill.

Moore, J. D. (1995). *Participating in explanatory dialogues: Interpreting and responding to questions in context*. Cambridge, MA: MIT Press.

Mueller, E. T. (2015). *Commonsense reasoning* (Second ed.). San Francisco: Morgan Kaufmann/Elsevier.

Quinlan, J. R. (1986). Induction of decision trees. *Machine Learning, 1*(1), 81–106.

Reiter, E., & Dale, R. (2000). *Building natural language generation systems*. Cambridge: Cambridge University Press.

Rips, L. J. (1994). *The psychology of proof: Deductive reasoning in human thinking*. Cambridge, MA: MIT Press.

Robinson, J. A., & Voronkov, A. (2001). *Handbook of automated reasoning* (Vol. 1 and 2). Amsterdam and Cambridge, MA: Elsevier and MIT Press.

Rumelhart, D. E., Smolensky, P., McClelland, J. L., & Hinton, G. E. (1986). Schemata and sequential thought processes in PDP models. In J. L. McClelland, D. E. Rumelhart, & PDP Research Group (Eds.), *Parallel distributed processing: Explorations in the microstructure of cognition* (Vol. 2: Psychological and Biological Models, pp. 7–57). Cambridge, MA: MIT Press.

Scott, A. C., Clancey, W. J., Davis, R., & Shortliffe, E. H. (1984). Methods for generating explanations. In B. G. Buchanan & E. H. Shortliffe (Eds.), *Rule-based expert systems: The MYCIN experiments of the Stanford Heuristic Programming Project* (pp. 338–362). Reading, MA: Addison-Wesley.

Simonyan, K., Vedaldi, A., & Zisserman, A. (2014). Deep inside convolutional networks: Visualising image classification models and saliency maps. In *Proceedings of the International Conference on Learning Representations (ICLR)*.

Stent, A., & Bangalore, S. (2014). *Natural language generation in interactive systems*. Cambridge: Cambridge University Press.

Tufte, E. R. (2001). *The visual display of quantitative information* (Second ed.). Cheshire, CT: Graphics Press.

Ungar, D., Lieberman, H., & Fry, C. (1997). Debugging and the experience of immediacy. *Communications of the ACM, 40(4)*, 38–43.

Weston, J., Bordes, A., Chopra, S., Rush, A. M., van Merriënboer, B., Joulin, A., & Mikolov, T. (2015). Towards AI-complete question answering: A set of prerequisite toy tasks. *Computing Research Repository, abs/1502.05698*. Retrieved from http://arxiv.org/abs/1502.05698

Wieland, C. (1990). *Two explanation facilities for the deductive database management system DeDEx* (Tech. Rep.). Zürich: Eidgenössische Technische Hochschule.

Yang, Z., He, X., Gao, J., Deng, L., & Smola, A. J. (2015). Stacked attention networks for image question answering. *Computing Research Repository, abs/1511.02274*. Retrieved from http://arxiv.org/abs/1511.02274

Author Index

Subject Index